Foreclosure Fight

What Banks Don't Tell You About Foreclosure In Massachusetts

By

Marc Saint Clair, MBA
© Copyright 2025

Disclaimer

The information presented in this book is intended for general educational and informational purposes only. While every effort has been made to ensure the accuracy and relevance of the content, foreclosure laws and legal procedures in Massachusetts are subject to change. Therefore, the author and publisher cannot guarantee the current applicability or accuracy of the information provided.

This book does not constitute legal advice or replace professional legal representation. Foreclosure proceedings involve complex legal processes that may significantly impact your rights and property. Readers are strongly encouraged to consult with a qualified attorney or legal professional before making any legal decisions or taking action. If you cannot afford legal representation, consider seeking free or low-cost legal aid services in your area.

The author and publisher disclaim any liability for any losses, damages, or legal consequences arising directly or indirectly from the use or application of the information in this book.

Acknowledgment

My name is Marc Saint Clair, and I have been in the real estate business since 2007 in the state of Massachusetts. During that time, I've helped many homeowners navigate the challenges of homeownership, but my passion for writing this book stems from a deeply personal experience. During a period of financial and family turbulence, I came dangerously close to losing my own home to foreclosure. That struggle opened my eyes to how vulnerable homeowners can be when facing banks and legal processes they barely understand.

I was moved to write this book to help others fighting to keep their homes. My goal is to empower readers with knowledge about foreclosure laws in Massachusetts, equipping them with practical tools and strategies to protect their rights.

I am immensely grateful to my wife, Veronique Saint Clair, for her unwavering support and encouragement throughout this project. Her belief in me has been my anchor.

Finally, I give thanks to Adonai, whose grace has carried me through every storm. It is my hope that this book will help homeowners fight back with confidence and stand a better chance of saving their homes.

Table of Contents

Massachusetts Foreclosure is Non-Judicial

The foreclosure process in Massachusetts is subtle and quick. **In Massachusetts, a mortgage foreclosure is non-judicial meaning that it happens without involvement of the courts.**

Chapter 1
What "Non-Judicial" Foreclosure Means

In Massachusetts, foreclosure is non-judicial, meaning you don't automatically get your day in court before losing your home. Many homeowners assume they will have the chance to fight foreclosure before a judge, but that only happens if you take legal action to bring the case into court yourself.

What "Non-Judicial" Foreclosure Means in Simple Terms:

- The bank does NOT have to sue you to foreclose.
- There is no court hearing before your home is sold.
- The lender follows a step-by-step process—giving notices, publishing the auction, and selling the property—without needing a judge's approval.

What This Means for You If You're Facing Foreclosure:

- You must take action to bring the fight to court. If you don't, the foreclosure will proceed without ever being reviewed by a judge.
- The best time to fight back is early! Waiting until after the auction makes it far more difficult to reverse the foreclosure.
- Legal options exist to stop foreclosure, but you need to act quickly.

Conversely, in a state with judicial foreclosure, the lender files a lawsuit in court to request permission to sell the home. If the homeowner does not respond, the lender automatically wins; if the homeowner contests, the court reviews the case and decides whether to allow the foreclosure.

Marc Saint Clair, MBA

Chapter 2
How It Starts

Many homeowners are caught off guard when they receive a 90-Day Right to Cure Notice, but the foreclosure process actually begins long before that letter arrives. The events leading up to the notice are just as critical, and understanding them can help you take action before things spiral out of control.

1. Missing Payments: The First Red Flag

Foreclosure begins with missed mortgage payments. Most lenders have a 15-day grace period after the due date. Once you pass this window without making your payment, the lender typically considers the loan delinquent.

- 30 Days Late: You'll likely receive a late payment notice and a late fee will be added to your account.
- 60 Days Late: You'll receive more serious collection calls and letters, urging you to bring the account current.
- 90 Days Late: This is when the lender begins the pre-foreclosure process. You're now considered in default, which triggers the lender's right to initiate foreclosure proceedings.

2. Pre-Foreclosure Notices and Lender Contact

Before issuing the official 90-Day Right to Cure Notice, lenders are required by law to make reasonable efforts to contact you and discuss loan modification options. Under Massachusetts General Laws Chapter 244, Section 35A, lenders must:

- Attempt to engage with you in good faith to explore alternatives (loan modifications, forbearance, etc.).
- Send a "Right to Request a Modified Mortgage Loan" notice at least 30 days before the 90-day cure notice.
- Provide information about counseling agencies and foreclosure prevention resources.

3. The Trigger: The 90-Day Right to Cure Notice

If no resolution is reached, the lender will issue the 90-Day Right to Cure Notice, which formally begins the foreclosure process. This notice gives you three months to bring the loan current.

During this period, you have the right to:

- Pay all missed payments and late fees to reinstate the loan.
- Seek loan modification or refinancing options.
- Dispute the debt if you believe the lender is in error.

If you fail to cure the default by the end of the 90 days, the lender can move forward with auctioning your property without needing a court's approval.

Massachusetts Foreclosure Roadmap and Timeline

Chapter 3
Right-To-Cure Period (Pre-Foreclosure)

After three consecutive months of late payments, Massachusetts law (Mass. Gen. Laws Ch. 244, § 35A) requires lenders to send a Right-to-Cure notice to the homeowner. This triggers a 90-day clock during which the borrower has the opportunity to catch up on missed payments and avoid foreclosure.

Required Elements of the Right-to-Cure Notice:

1. **Borrower and Lender Information:**
   o Full legal names of the borrower and lender.
   o Property address.
   o Lender's address and servicer's details (if handled by a third party).

2. **Statement of Default:**
   o Clear notification of mortgage default due to missed payments.
   o Specifies the amount required to cure the default, including:
   - Past-due principal, interest, late fees, and penalties.
   - Escrow shortages (if applicable).
   - The total amount required to bring the loan current.

3. **Deadline to Cure the Default:**
   - A clear statement specifying the 90-day period to cure the default.
   - The exact date the Right-to-Cure period expires.
   - Notice that the borrower is entitled to only one Right-to-Cure notice every five years.

4. **Consequences of Non-Payment:**
   - Explanation that failure to cure by the deadline will initiate foreclosure proceedings.
   - Notification that the lender may accelerate the loan, making the full balance due immediately.

5. **Payment Instructions:**
   - Detailed instructions on how to make the payment, including:
     - Address or servicer details.
     - Toll-free number for verifying the amount or disputing the notice.

6. **Borrower's Rights and Options:**
   - Notice of the borrower's right to consult with legal counsel or a housing counselor.
   - Specific reference to MassHousing and the Division of Banks (DOB), with contact information.
   - Notification that the borrower may qualify for a loan modification or forbearance plan.

7. **Other Required Information:**
   - Borrower may sell the property prior to foreclosure and use the proceeds to pay off the mortgage.
   - Borrower may redeem the property by paying the total due before the foreclosure sale.
   - Notice of potential eviction after foreclosure.
   - Explanation of the borrower's rights to:
     - Refinance the loan to fully repay the debt.
     - Grant a deed in lieu of foreclosure to the lender.

- o A declaration on the first page stating:
  - "This is an important notice concerning your right to live in your home."

8. **Compliance with Federal and State Regulations:**
   - o The notice must comply with Massachusetts and federal laws regarding foreclosure proceedings.

9. **Language Requirements (if applicable):**
   - o If the borrower has requested mortgage correspondence in a language other than English, the lender must provide the Right-to-Cure notice in the requested language or include a translated statement directing the borrower to translation services.

10. **Compliance with Federal and State Regulations:**
    - o The notice must comply with Massachusetts and federal laws regarding foreclosure proceedings.

11. **Other Requirements:**
    - o The Right-to-Cure notice must be sent by certified or registered mail with return receipt requested.
    - o The borrower is not responsible for any attorney fees incurred by the lender prior to the 90-day notice period and during the 90-day right to cure period.

12. **According to MA section 59, chapter 183, lenders may only charge a maximum of:**
    - o 3% of the overdue principal and interest **after the** 15-day grace period.
    - o No late fees on escrow items (property taxes, insurance).

13. **Some loans with high fees and interest rates, hidden balloon payments among other features are covered by MGL Chapter 244, Section 35B(c):**

o Must include borrower's right to pursue loan modification.

Steps to Take to Avert Foreclosure at this stage:

Contact Your Lender Immediately:

- Request a loan modification, forbearance, or repayment plan.
- Depending on your lender and communication efforts, you may be able to negotiate a 30-90 day extension.
- Even if you feel the situation is hopeless, ask for more time—some lenders are more flexible than expected.

Increase Your Income or Seek Financial Assistance:

- Take on an extra job if feasible.
- Seek financial assistance from family, friends, place of worship, or community organizations.
- Lenders often prefer reinstatement over foreclosure, as it is more cost-effective for them.
- Demonstrating your willingness to bring the account current could work in your favor.

Apply for Mortgage Payment Assistance:

- Massachusetts offers mortgage assistance programs. Apply here: MassHousing Assistance

  https://applyhousinghelp.mass.gov
  Once you create a profile, start a Residential Assistance for Families in Transition (RAFT) application action.

- The first set of questions will be about your living situation. Click on "Homeowner living in the home." On the same page, you will have the option to include an advocate. If you are working with a foreclosure prevention advisor, it is recommended that you enter their information there. You can then continue providing your own information.

- As of today, this program can give you up to $7,000 if you qualify. Income restriction applies (50% of area median income).

As of 2024, the 50% AMI income limits for the Boston-Cambridge-Quincy, MA-NH HUD Metro FMR Area are as follows:
- One-person household: $57,150
- Two-person household: $65,300
- Three-person household: $73,450
- Four-person household: $81,600
- Five-person household: $88,150
- Six-person household: $94,700

If your household income exceeds that amount, you would not qualify.

401K Hardship Withdrawal:

- If permitted, consider making a hardship withdrawal from your 401K to pay the outstanding amount.
- Note: This is subject to income tax and, if you are under 59.5 years old, a 10% early withdrawal penalty.

Seek Housing Counseling: A counselor can help negotiate a solution or apply for loss mitigation programs.

- Consult with a HUD-certified housing counselor or legal aid organization for guidance on loan workouts or mediation.
- Shortlist of some organizations in MA that came under my radar in the past. If they don't work in your area, they might be able to give you a referral for another organization in your area:

- 617-479-8181 Quincy Community Action Program
- 617-770-2227 Neighborhood Housing Services

Foreclosure Fight

- 617-573-5333 HomeCorps Hotline
- 617-889-2277 Chelsea Restoration Corporation
- 617-787-9804 Midas Collaborative

Consider Selling the Home (if feasible):

If you're considering selling your home to avoid foreclosure, hiring a qualified real estate agent is essential. An experienced agent can help you explore all available options, including whether a short sale (selling for less than the remaining mortgage balance) or a traditional sale would be more beneficial. They can market the property effectively, and maximize your chances of getting the best possible outcome.

- If you're struggling to keep up with mortgage payments, it may be time to explore whether selling is a viable option.
- Start evaluating the market with your real estate agent: Research your home's current value and assess whether selling could allow you to pay off the mortgage and potentially have funds left over to relocate
- Consult with the real estate agent to understand your home's fair market value and get an estimate of sale proceeds.
- Why consider this? Selling your home before foreclosure can:
  - Help you avoid the negative impact of foreclosure on your credit.
  - Give you more control over the process and potentially preserve your equity.
  - Provide funds to transition to a more affordable living situation.
  - **This should be a last-resort consideration only if keeping the home is no longer feasible**.

Consider Bankruptcy (Last Resort):

- Filing for bankruptcy can temporarily halt foreclosure:
  - Chapter 13 Bankruptcy: Pauses foreclosure and sets up a repayment plan.
  - Chapter 7 Bankruptcy: Temporarily delays foreclosure and may eliminate other debts.
- Upon filing, the court issues an automatic stay, which immediately stops foreclosure proceedings.

Other Creative Ideas:

- Rent a room in the house, if possible, to generate extra income.
- Leverage Massachusetts' Additional Dwelling Unit (ADU) Law:
  Under Massachusetts General Laws Chapter 40A, Section 3, you can convert part of your basement, attic, garage, or a section of an existing structure into an additional dwelling unit (ADU). If you are financially able, making minor changes to the property can allow you to formally rent to a tenant and create a steady income stream
- If financially feasible, you can temporarily move out and rent your home if family and friends can graciously host you for a year. This strategy is only viable if the rental income covers your mortgage and expenses. However, it comes with the risk of dealing with unreliable tenants who could complicate your financial situation. Consider tenants on government-subsidized housing programs, as the government pays on time, reducing the risk of late or missed payments.

Key Takeaway:
The Right-to-Cure period is a critical window during which homeowners have the opportunity to save their property. By understanding their rights, acting quickly, and exploring available assistance programs, borrowers can potentially avoid foreclosure and retain ownership of their home. This protection specifically

Foreclosure Fight

applies to owner-occupied residential properties with 1-4 units, not investment properties

Marc Saint Clair, MBA

Chapter 4
Notice of Mortgage Default

After the 90-Day Right-to-Cure period expires, the lender will take the next legal steps to initiate foreclosure. Depending on the lender's process, Chapter 4 and Chapter 5 may occur simultaneously or separately.

What Is a Notice of Mortgage Default?

If the homeowner has not resolved the default during the right-to-cure period, the lender or their attorney will issue a Notice of Mortgage Default. This formal letter notifies the borrower that foreclosure proceedings are beginning.

The lender may also send a demand letter, known as a Notice of Acceleration, if no action is taken. Some lenders combine the Notice of Mortgage Default and Notice of Acceleration into a single letter, while others issue them separately as part of their internal process.

Timeline and Legal Considerations

The timeframe from receiving the Notice of Mortgage Default to a potential foreclosure auction typically ranges from 4 to 6 months, but this can vary significantly due to:

- Court filings (e.g., legal challenges or foreclosure defense cases).
- Loan modification applications or other loss mitigation efforts.
- Bankruptcy filings, which can delay or temporarily halt the foreclosure process.

Foreclosure Fight

What This Means for Homeowners

- This notice serves as the lender's final warning before moving forward with foreclosure.
- It confirms that the homeowner is officially in default and at risk of losing their property.
- If no action is taken, the lender will proceed with the Notice of Acceleration, demanding full repayment of the remaining loan balance.

Steps to Take to Avert Foreclosure at this stage:

Contact Your Lender Immediately:

- Request a loan modification, forbearance, or repayment plan. Many lenders are willing to work with homeowners to avoid the costly foreclosure process.

Seek Financial Assistance:

- Ask family, friends, social networks, or religious communities for temporary financial support.
- Even partial payments could demonstrate good faith and potentially buy you time.

Consult a HUD-Certified Housing Counselor:

- A HUD-approved counselor can help you understand your options and negotiate alternatives with your lender.

Explore Legal Options:

- Contact a foreclosure defense attorney to evaluate potential legal claims, lender violations, or negotiation strategies.

Consider Selling Your Home:

- If foreclosure seems imminent, selling the home may be a viable option.
- Keep in mind that foreclosed properties typically sell for 20-30% below market value due to associated fees and discounts.
- If the lender sells the house for more than you owe (a surplus) after the foreclosure, it belongs to you, but you must actively claim it—it will not be automatically disbursed.

Bankruptcy as a Last Resort:

- Filing for Chapter 13 or Chapter 7 bankruptcy may temporarily halt foreclosure proceedings. Consult with a qualified attorney to understand the potential benefits and risks.

Key Takeaway:

Receiving a Notice of Mortgage Default is a critical turning point in the foreclosure process. It serves as the lender's final warning before accelerating the loan and moving forward with foreclosure proceedings. Homeowners still have options at this stage—by acting quickly, seeking financial assistance, and exploring legal or loan modification solutions, they may be able to prevent foreclosure and protect their home.

Chapter 5
Notice of Acceleration

O
nce the Notice of Mortgage Default is issued, the lender may proceed with a Notice of Acceleration and Intent to Foreclose. This chapter outlines the next steps in the foreclosure process and the homeowner's remaining options.

What Is a Notice of Acceleration?

If the default is not resolved, the lender's attorney will issue a Notice of Acceleration. In Massachusetts, while state law does not explicitly require a separate acceleration notice, most lenders comply with the terms of the mortgage contract, which typically mandates notice before accelerating the loan balance.

Some lenders issue this notice shortly after the Notice of Mortgage Default, while others send both simultaneously. The lender's internal legal strategy or the specific mortgage agreement terms determine the approach.

Key Points About the Notice of Acceleration

The timeframe from receiving the Notice of Mortgage Default to a potential foreclosure auction typically ranges from 4 to 6 months, but this can vary significantly due to:

- It formally demands full repayment of the remaining loan balance (not just the past-due amounts).
- The letter outlines all previous foreclosure steps and confirms that the homeowner has not resolved the default.

- It provides instructions for requesting a payoff amount and may offer a final opportunity to communicate with the lender.

What This Means for Homeowners

- The lender is now seeking immediate repayment of the entire loan balance, not just missed payments.
- The foreclosure process will escalate if no action is taken.
- This is typically the final notice before the bank proceeds with legal action, including filing for a foreclosure sale.

Steps to Take to Avert Foreclosure at this stage:

At this stage, time is critical. Homeowners must act quickly to prevent further escalation.

Contact Your Lender Immediately

- Request a payoff statement and explore possible reinstatement options.

Seek Financial Assistance

Consult a HUD-Certified Housing Counselor

Explore Legal Options:

- Engage a foreclosure defense attorney to assess any legal violations or to negotiate on your behalf.
- Attorneys can sometimes delay or halt the foreclosure process through legal challenges.

Consider Selling Your Home:

- If you can sell the property, it may help you avoid foreclosure and protect your credit.
- Be aware that:
  - Foreclosed homes typically sell at a significant discount (20-30% below market value).
  - If the sale price exceeds the mortgage balance, you are entitled to the surplus.
  - If you owe more than the home is worth, explore the possibility of a short sale, which is generally less damaging to your credit than a full foreclosure.
- However, selling should be a last resort, as finding new housing may be difficult.
- Rental prices are often substantially higher than existing mortgage payments, which could strain your finances further.

Short Sale Explained

A short sale occurs when you sell your home for less than what you owe on the mortgage, with your lender's approval. This option can help you avoid foreclosure, but you will lose the home. The process involves finding a buyer, negotiating a sale price, and obtaining the lender's consent to accept less than the full loan amount. While a short sale damages your credit, it is typically less harmful than a foreclosure.

Keep in mind that short sales require lender approval, which can take weeks or months. Additionally, the lender may either forgive the remaining balance or pursue you for the difference through a deficiency judgment. You won't profit from the sale, and the forgiven debt could be considered taxable income, potentially leading to a tax bill—so it's wise to consult with a tax professional

Bankruptcy as a Last Resort

After issuing the Notice of Acceleration, the lender's attorneys will typically consult with the bank regarding the next steps. In most cases, they recommend proceeding with the Land Court process. However, if you effectively communicate with your lender, demonstrate financial hardship, and express a genuine effort to catch up on payments, they may instruct their attorneys to delay the process temporarily.

At this stage, proactive communication is your most powerful tool. Work diligently with your lender, explore all possible alternatives, and seek professional legal and financial guidance to improve your chances of avoiding foreclosure.

Chapter 6
Foreclosure Protection for Military Members Under SCRA in MA

The Servicemembers Civil Relief Act (SCRA) provides vital foreclosure protections for active-duty military personnel, safeguarding them from losing their homes while serving. In Massachusetts, lenders are required to initiate an SCRA case in Land Court or Superior Court to verify whether the homeowner qualifies for these protections. This ensures that servicemembers receive the legal safeguards they are entitled to before foreclosure can proceed.

Timeline: Throughout foreclosure proceedings (from pre-foreclosure to post-sale).

Lenders initiate an SCRA case in Land Court to confirm whether a homeowner is an active-duty military member eligible for foreclosure protections. The goal is to ensure lenders comply with federal law protections for servicemembers before proceeding with foreclosure.

Procedure:

1. Order of Notice Issued:

- o The court issues an Order of Notice, which is recorded at the Registry of Deeds.

2. Homeowner Notification:
   - o Homeowners receive a formal complaint notifying them of the SCRA case.
   - o They have 20–30 days to respond.

3. Default Judgment:
   - o If the homeowner fails to respond, the lender can obtain a default judgment, declaring the borrower ineligible for SCRA protections.
   - o This allows the lender to proceed with foreclosure without further legal barriers.

Protection by Military Status:

1. Active Duty:
   - o Foreclosure is prohibited without a court order during active duty and for 12 months post-service.
   - o Interest rates are capped at 6% during service and for 1 year afterward.

2. Reserves/National Guard:
   - o Protected only if on active-duty orders during foreclosure proceedings.

3. Veterans:
   - o No protections unless within 12 months of leaving active duty.

Options to Prevent Foreclosure:

For Active-Duty Servicemembers:

- File an Answer to the SCRA Complaint:

Foreclosure Fight

- o Submitting a response within 20–30 days triggers automatic foreclosure delays, buying you more time.

- Request Interest Rate Reduction:
  - o Under the SCRA, you can request your mortgage interest rate to be retroactively capped at 6% during your service and for one year post-service.

- Contact Legal Support:
  - o Seek assistance from JAG (Judge Advocate General) or Armed Forces Legal Assistance for free legal support.

Key Takeaway:

The Servicemembers Civil Relief Act (SCRA) offers crucial protections for active-duty military members facing foreclosure in Massachusetts. By filing an SCRA case, lenders must confirm whether the homeowner is entitled to these protections before proceeding. Active-duty servicemembers can benefit from foreclosure delays, reduced interest rates, and access to free legal support, helping them safeguard their homes while serving their country.

Chapter 7
Lender Files Servicemembers Civil Relief Act (SCRA)

The Servicemembers Civil Relief Act (SCRA) is a federal law designed to protect active-duty military personnel from certain legal actions, including foreclosure, while they are serving. In Massachusetts, lenders are required to file an SCRA petition in Land Court to verify whether the homeowner is on active military duty. This legal step ensures that eligible servicemembers receive temporary foreclosure protection.

Once the lender instructs their attorney to proceed, the petition is filed. This process determines if the homeowner qualifies for SCRA protections, which can delay or prevent foreclosure during active service.

Timeline: Within days of the Notice of Acceleration.

Why This Matters
Homeowners often misunderstand this stage and believe that filing a written response to the SCRA petition will delay foreclosure or bring their defenses into court. Unfortunately, this is not the case. Based on recent communication with the Land Court, we've confirmed that unless you file a separate lawsuit (known as a "Complaint") in Land Court or Superior Court, your objections or defenses will not be considered.

Foreclosure Fight

Key Actions in This Stage:

- The lender's attorney files the SCRA petition with the Massachusetts Land Court.
- The court reviews the homeowner's military status to confirm if they are protected under the SCRA.
- If applicable, the homeowner receives a Land Court summons, officially notifying them of the proceeding.

Steps to Take to Avert Foreclosure at this stage:

Check if You Qualify for SCRA Protection:

- If you are an active-duty service member, you may be eligible for temporary protection from foreclosure under the SCRA. You may be protected from foreclosure during service + 12 months post-service. Consult a Judge Advocate General (JAG) immediately to understand your rights and file the necessary legal responses.
- Filing an "Answer" to the SCRA petition without a formal complaint will likely lead to a default judgment, allowing the foreclosure to proceed.

File a separate complaint:

If you believe your lender has violated Massachusetts foreclosure laws, you must take additional legal action to raise those issues:

- File a Verified Complaint in Land Court or Superior Court outlining the violations.

Request a Temporary Restraining Order (TRO) or Injunction:

- You or your attorney can file a motion for a TRO or injunction to halt the foreclosure temporarily.

- This can give you more time to negotiate a resolution with the lender or explore legal remedies.
- List all relevant defenses:

  - Improper Notice: The lender failed to send the required notices.
  - Foreclosure Violations: The lender did not comply with Massachusetts foreclosure laws.
  - Missing Documentation: The lender cannot provide the necessary mortgage or assignment records.
  - Improper Loan Assignments: Issues with Mortgage Electronic Registration Systems (MERS) transfers, if applicable.

You are not required to have an attorney, but hiring one greatly increases your chances. If you cannot afford one, seek free legal help through:

- Volunteer Lawyers Project (www.vlpnet.org)
- Greater Boston Legal Services
- Local legal aid organizations

In Massachusetts, when a foreclosure notice is filed in Land Court under the Servicemembers Civil Relief Act (SCRA), there is a return date listed on the notice.

What is the Return Date?

The return date is the deadline for the homeowner to respond to the foreclosure case in Land Court. It is not a court hearing date but simply the last day for you to file an answer or response if you want to contest the foreclosure based on military status or other legal grounds.

What Happens by the Return Date?

- If you are on active military duty, responding by the return date could give you protections under the Servicemembers Civil Relief Act (SCRA), which may delay the foreclosure.

Key Takeaway:

Responding to the SCRA petition alone is not enough. To assert your legal defenses or slow foreclosure, you must file a separate complaint in Land Court or Superior Court. This extra step is your opportunity to preserve your rights, challenge improper practices, and potentially stop or delay foreclosure.

To assist you, I have included a **Sample Response Letter** that you can customize and submit to the Massachusetts Land Court. This letter is designed to help you raise potential defenses, preserve your rights, and slow down the foreclosure process.

Please review the sample carefully, adjust it based on your situation, and delete any defenses that do not apply.

Where to file: Land Court or Superior Court

Commonwealth of Massachusetts
Land Court Department
Three Pemberton Square, Boston, MA 02108

Docket No. (To be assigned)
[Your Name], Plaintiff
[Bank or Mortgage Holder's Name], Defendant.

VERIFIED COMPLAINT TO PREVENT WRONGFUL FORECLOSURE SALE

INTRODUCTION

1.   Plaintiff, **[Your Full Name]**, brings this action to halt an imminent foreclosure auction scheduled for **[Date]**, asserting violations of Massachusetts foreclosure law and procedural irregularities.

PARTIES

2.   The plaintiff is a resident of **[Full Address]** and the owner of the subject property.
3.   Defendant is **[Bank Name or Mortgage Servicer]**, located at **[Defendant's Address]**, servicing or owning the subject mortgage.

JURISDICTION AND VENUE

4.   Jurisdiction is proper under G.L. c. 185, § 1(k), and venue lies in this court as the property is located in Massachusetts.

FACTUAL ALLEGATIONS

5.   Plaintiff is the record owner of property located at **[Address]** since **[Date]**.
6.   A foreclosure auction is currently scheduled for **[Date]** by Defendant.

Plaintiff alleges procedural and legal deficiencies in the foreclosure process, including but not limited to:

Foreclosure Fight

[**Please read carefully and remove any defenses that do not apply. Delete any defenses that do not apply to your case. Keep anything that you reasonably believe applies.**]

1. **Failure to Properly Serve Notices:**
   - I did not receive the required Right-to-Cure Notice (Mass. Gen. Laws Ch. 244 § 35A) in a timely manner, either by certified mail or hand delivery.
2. **Lack of good faith effort to modify the loan (§ 35B);**
3. **Premature SCRA filing or errors in the notice**.
4. **Defective Right-to-Cure Notice:**
   - The 90-day Right-to-Cure Notice did not contain all the required disclosures (such as housing counseling information, division or Bank or language translation notice) per Massachusetts law.
5. **Violation of 90-Day Cure Period:**
   - The lender accelerated the loan or proceeded with foreclosure before the expiration of the full 90-day cure period.
6. **Failure to File Notice with Division of Banks:**
   - The lender failed to properly file the required notice with the Division of Banks (as mandated by § 35A(f)).
7. **No Good Faith Effort to Modify Loan (35B Violation):**
   - The lender did not make a good faith effort to offer a loan modification as required under Mass. Gen. Laws Ch. 244 § 35B.
8. **Defective Mortgage Assignment:**
   - The lender does not hold proper assignment of the mortgage at the time of the foreclosure notice.
9. **Improper mortgage assignment or missing promissory note.**
10. **Missing Endorsements or Note:**
    - The original promissory note is missing, improperly endorsed, or not held by the lender (UCC enforcement issues).

11. **MERS (Mortgage Electronic Registration Systems) Errors:**
    o The foreclosure involves a MERS assignment, and the lender failed to prove proper standing under Massachusetts case law (e.g., Eaton v. Federal National Mortgage Association).

12. **Predatory Loan Practices:**
    o The original loan involved predatory terms such as adjustable rates, no-income verification, or hidden balloon payments covered under 35B protections.

13. **Violation of Massachusetts Consumer Protection Laws (Ch. 93A):**
    o The lender engaged in unfair or deceptive practices in servicing or foreclosing the loan.

14. **Improper Notice of Sale Publication:**
    o The foreclosure sale notice was not published in a local newspaper for three consecutive weeks, as required by law.

15. **Failure to Provide Proper Payoff or Reinstatement Figures:**
    o The lender refused to provide accurate payoff amounts despite requests, hindering my ability to cure the default.

16. **Servicemembers Petition Premature:**
    o The lender filed the Servicemembers Civil Relief Act Petition before completing mandatory pre-foreclosure steps.

17. **Unfair Late Fees or Charges:**
    o The lender charged late fees or penalties inconsistent with Massachusetts law (Mass. Gen. Laws Ch. 183 § 59).

18. **Failure to Acknowledge Ongoing Loan Modification Review:**
    o I submitted a loss mitigation application, and the lender proceeded with foreclosure during active review (dual tracking violation).

Based on the above, I respectfully request that:

- The Court requires strict proof of compliance with all applicable foreclosure statutes and federal protections.
- Any defects or violations be reviewed before proceeding with foreclosure actions.
- My rights be preserved to raise additional defenses and claims as discovery proceeds.

Thank you for your consideration.

CAUSES OF ACTION
Count I – Imminent Wrongful Foreclosure
Count II – Violation of G.L. c. 244, §§ 14, 35A, 35B
Count III – Declaratory Relief & Quiet Title

RELIEF REQUESTED
A. Temporarily enjoin the foreclosure auction; B. Declare pending auction unlawful until proper process is followed; C. Quiet title in Plaintiff's name until proper resolution; D. Grant any additional relief deemed appropriate.

Respectfully submitted,
[Your Name]
[Signature]
[Phone Number]
[Email Address]
[Date]

MOTION FOR TEMPORARY RESTRAINING ORDER (TRO) / PRELIMINARY INJUNCTION

Plaintiff respectfully requests the Court issue an emergency TRO and preliminary injunction to stop the foreclosure auction scheduled for **[Date]**.

Grounds:
1. Property auction will cause irreparable harm.
2. Defenses raised suggest significant legal violations.
3. Balance of equities favors Plaintiff.
4. Public interest supports due process.

AFFIDAVIT IN SUPPORT OF MOTION FOR INJUNCTION

I, **[Your Name]**, declare under oath:
1. I reside at and own **[Property Address]**.
2. The property is scheduled for auction on **[Date]**.
3. I did not receive proper notice, modification efforts were not offered, and/or the lender has violated Massachusetts foreclosure procedures.
4. I face loss of home, homelessness, and health hardship if auction occurs.

Signed under the pains and penalties of perjury,

Date: _____

[Your Full Name]
[Address]
[Phone]
[Email]

PROPOSED ORDER
Commonwealth of Massachusetts
Land Court Department
[Your Name], Plaintiff
v.
[Bank], Defendant

The Court hereby ORDERS:
1.   Defendant shall immediately CEASE any action to proceed with foreclosure auction of **[Address]**.
2.   No transfer or sale of the deed shall occur until further order of this Court.

SO ORDERED,

Justice of the Land Court

Date: _____

SERVICE INSTRUCTIONS
1.   File Document at land court or superior court.
   - Verified Complaint & Motion for Temporary Restraining Order (TRO): File at Land Court.
   - Obtain formal summons from the clerk.

2.   Serve all parties:
   - Deliver the Summons, Verified Complaint, TRO motion, and supporting documents to:
        The lender or bank
        The mortgage servicer
        Any listed foreclosure attorneys

3.   Acceptable method of service:
   - Sheriffs Office

- Constable
- Certified mail with return receipt requested (If permitted by court)

4. Save Your Proofs

- Keep:
    - A stamped court filing receipt (if filing in person) or
    - USPS Certified Mail tracking receipts.

Deadline Reminder:

You have the right to defend your home.

Now that you understand how to respond to the Servicemembers Civil Relief Act (SCRA) petition, it's equally important to know what happens next. In the following chapter, we'll walk you through what to expect after you submit your response, how the court and the lender typically proceed, and what additional steps you can take to protect your rights and delay or stop the foreclosure process.

Important Update on Veteran Mortgage Assistance

As of May 1, 2025, the Department of Veterans Affairs (VA) has concluded the Veterans Affairs Servicing Purchase (VASP) program. This initiative was established to assist veterans facing financial hardships by allowing the VA to purchase delinquent loans and offer modified terms, including reduced interest rates, to help prevent foreclosures. With the program's conclusion, veterans seeking mortgage relief will need to explore alternative options, such as contacting their loan servicers for available loss mitigation programs or seeking assistance from housing counselors. It's crucial for affected individuals to act promptly to understand their rights and available resources to safeguard their homes.

Chapter 8
What Happens After You Take Legal Action

Facing a foreclosure is overwhelming, but taking early legal action—whether you're a veteran responding to the Servicemembers Civil Relief Act (SCRA) Petition, or a homeowner filing a formal Complaint and Temporary Restraining Order (TRO) is a critical step toward defending your home.

This chapter explains what happens after your paperwork is filed with the Massachusetts Land Court.

If You Filed a Response to the SCRA Petition (Veterans)

Veterans covered by the SCRA may file a direct response to the petition. Once your response is received:

- The Land Court will log your answer and notify the lender's attorney.
- You may or may not get a hearing, but the court may review your case more closely if you raised:
  - Improper notice
  - Violations of Massachusetts foreclosure law
  - SCRA protections or lender misconduct

If You Filed a Formal Complaint & TRO (Non-Veterans or All Homeowners)

If you are not a servicemember, your foreclosure challenge must be done by filing a Verified Complaint along with a Motion for a TRO or Preliminary Injunction. Here's what typically happens next:

- The court will review your Complaint and motion and may schedule a hearing on the TRO.
- You may receive written questions (orders) or instructions from the court for more information.
- The lender will be formally served and must respond or appear in court.
- If granted, the TRO will temporarily halt the foreclosure auction or further legal steps.

Possible Outcomes After Filing

Here are the most common outcomes after filing your response:

Outcome	What It Means	Next Steps
No Immediate Hearing	Your case is filed, and foreclosure is temporarily paused	Monitor mail and docket. Begin preparing additional legal motions or defenses.
Court Requests More Information	You may be asked for additional documentation or clarity	Respond by the deadline. Consider legal aid or housing attorney support.
TRO Hearing is Scheduled	You'll present your case before a judge	Prepare documents and evidence. Attend the hearing.
Lender Amends or Cancels Action	Lender may recognize defects and pause or fix issues	Use the extra time to negotiate or seek a loan modification.

Critical Actions After Filing

• Check Your Mail Daily: Court notices, orders, and updates are usually sent by mail.

Foreclosure Fight

- Save all records, including certified mail receipts, stamped copies from the court, and your complaint.

- Track Deadlines: Missing any deadlines could allow the foreclosure to proceed by default.

- Continue Defending Your Home:

    - If you filed a TRO, follow up with the court and prepare for a potential hearing.
    - Explore legal assistance or nonprofit mediation programs.

Key Takeaway:
Filing a response to the SCRA petition (if you're a veteran) or submitting a formal Complaint and TRO (for all homeowners) is not the end—it's just the beginning of your foreclosure defense. These actions can pause the process, put pressure on the lender, and give you precious time to seek resolution, whether that's a modification, settlement, or another path forward.
Stay vigilant, respond quickly, and use every available resource to protect your home.

Chapter 9
Notice of Foreclosure Sale & Pubic Advertising

At this stage of the foreclosure process, the lender is required to provide formal notice of the foreclosure auction to the homeowner and the public. This includes sending a certified letter to the borrower and advertising the auction in a local newspaper, giving the homeowner one last opportunity to take action before the property is sold.

Key Actions in This Stage:

- **Foreclosure Auction Notice**: At least 14 days before the auction, the borrower must receive the certified notice.

- **Public Notice**: The lender must advertise the auction in a local newspaper for three consecutive weeks, starting at least 21 days before the foreclosure sale

Key Actions in This Stage:

- The lender sends a certified letter to the homeowner, notifying them of the foreclosure auction date.
- The lender publishes the sale notice in a newspaper for public awareness.
- The sale notice includes:
  - The date, time, and location of the foreclosure auction.
  - A description of the property and terms of sale.

Foreclosure Fight

Steps to Take to Avert Foreclosure at this stage:

Call the Massachusetts Division of Banks:

- Contact the Division of Banks at 617-956-1501 within 7 business days before the auction.
- This program is staffed mostly by volunteers.
- It may help delay the auction by up to 60 days.
- Important: This assistance is usually granted only once. Second-time borrowers are rarely successful in obtaining another delay.
- The earlier you call within the 7-day window, the better your chances of intervention.

Work with Real Estate Agent to attempt to sell the property

Negotiate with Your Lender:

- Even at this late stage, you can attempt to negotiate for a loan modification or refinancing.
- Some lenders may agree to a last-minute modification, particularly if you can show proof of funds or demonstrate that you are actively seeking financial assistance

Consider Bankruptcy as a Last Resort.

- Filing for Chapter 13 or Chapter 7 bankruptcy may temporarily halt the foreclosure.
- Chapter 13 bankruptcy: Allows you to pause the foreclosure and establish a repayment plan. This can help you catch up on overdue payments over time.
- Chapter 7 bankruptcy: May delay the process temporarily but could result in liquidation of assets.

- Consult with a bankruptcy attorney to evaluate whether this option is right for you.

Key Takeaway:

Time is running out at this stage. Calling the Division of Banks is one of the most effective last-minute strategies to delay the foreclosure auction. Simultaneously, explore short sales, loan modifications, or legal interventions.

Chapter 10
Foreclosure Auction (Non-Judicial Foreclosure)

The foreclosure auction is the final stage in the process, where the property is sold to the highest bidder—either on-site or online. This sale typically occurs 22-45 days after the foreclosure notice is published.

• The foreclosure auction is held either on-site at the property or online, where the home is sold to the highest bidder.

• In many cases, the lender purchases the property at the auction if no higher bids are made.

• Alternatively, a third party (such as an investor) may buy the home

Steps to Take to Avert Foreclosure at this stage:

File for Bankruptcy

Seek Emergency Legal Intervention – Some homeowners may have grounds to stop the sale due to procedural errors or improper notice. Consult with a foreclosure defense attorney immediately to determine if you can request an injunction.

Secure Last-Minute Funding – Explore emergency funding options from:

• Private lenders who offer short-term loans.

- Nonprofit housing assistance programs that may provide relief to cover missed payments.
- Friends or family who may be willing to lend financial support.

Key Takeaway:
Once the auction date is scheduled, time is critical. Your last line of defense is to either trigger an automatic stay through bankruptcy or seek emergency legal intervention. If you can raise funds quickly through private or nonprofit sources, you may still be able to save your home. Act swiftly once the auction occurs, your ownership rights are just about lost.

Chapter 11
Post-Foreclosure

After the foreclosure auction, the new owner—whether the lender or a third-party buyer—will typically move quickly to gain full control of the property. Their goal is to remove the former homeowner as quickly and cheaply as possible. This often involves filing for eviction proceedings within 30-90 days to take legal possession of the home.

What to Expect After Foreclosure:

- You may receive a "cash-for-keys" offer, where the new owner offers the previous owner a cash payment in exchange for voluntarily leaving the property.
- If you refuse to leave, the new owner can start legal process to request a court order for eviction.

Cash for Keys Explained:

Cash for Keys is a common tactic used by investors or new property owners to avoid the lengthy and costly eviction process. In this arrangement:

- The new owner offers you cash in exchange for a voluntary move-out.
- This benefits both parties—the new owner avoids legal fees and potential property damage, while you receive money to assist with moving expenses or secure new housing. If the previous home owner is contesting the foreclosure, it can take as much as 6-12 months

- If you receive eviction notices, a Cash for Keys deal, might be on its way to you.
- Get everything in writing. I have seen situations where people request that the payment funds are transferred to a third party.

Steps to Take to Avert Eviction:

Negotiate a Lease-Back Agreement – Some new owners, particularly investors, may be open to allowing you to rent the home instead of evicting you. This is known as a lease-back agreement.

Propose a Cash for Keys Deal – If you can't stay, try negotiating a cash-for-keys agreement. This can give you funds to help with relocation costs.

Seek Relocation Assistance – Contact Massachusetts housing programs to inquire about relocation grants or temporary housing assistance.

Challenge the Foreclosure in Court – Although extremely difficult at this stage, you can attempt to challenge the foreclosure sale in court if you have evidence of:

- Legal violations (e.g., improper notice, predatory lending practices).
- Lender misconduct during the foreclosure process.
- Errors in the sale procedure.

Key Takeaway:
After the auction, your focus shifts to protecting your rights and negotiating the best possible outcome. If eviction is looming, consider negotiating a cash-for-keys deal or lease-back arrangement to buy time and secure financial support. Even after the sale, legal challenges are possible in cases of foreclosure errors or violations, but they require swift legal action.

Chapter 12
Filing for Bankruptcy Without an Attorney

Filing for Chapter 7 or Chapter 13 bankruptcy without an attorney known as "pro se" filing is legal but can be complex and risky. In Massachusetts, pro se filers must submit their petitions in person or by mail at the U.S. Bankruptcy Court for the District of Massachusetts. Electronic filing (e-filing) is only available to attorneys, making it more challenging for individuals to file efficiently.

Although you have the right to file without an attorney, it is strongly recommended to seek legal counsel or assistance from free legal aid services. Bankruptcy laws and procedures are complicated, and even small mistakes can result in dismissal or loss of important protections. However, if you decide to proceed pro se, this chapter outlines the necessary steps, tips, and resources to help you succeed.

Where to File for Bankruptcy in Massachusetts (Pro Se)

The U.S. Bankruptcy Court for the District of Massachusetts has three locations where you can file:

1. **Boston Division (Eastern Division)**
   John W. McCormack Post Office and Courthouse
   5 Post Office Square, Suite 1150
   Boston, MA 02109-3945
   (617) 748-5300
   Jurisdiction: Suffolk, Bristol, Essex, Middlesex, Norfolk, and Plymouth counties

2. **Worcester Division (Central Division)**
   Donohue Federal Building and Courthouse
   595 Main Street
   Worcester, MA 01608-2076
   (508) 770-8900
   Jurisdiction: Worcester, Franklin, Hampden, Hampshire, and Berkshire counties
3. **Springfield Division (Western Division)**
   U.S. Courthouse
   300 State Street, Suite 220
   Springfield, MA 01105
   (413) 785-6900
   Jurisdiction: Hampshire, Hampden, Franklin, and Berkshire counties

Online Filing: Only for Attorneys

- The Massachusetts Bankruptcy Court uses the CM/ECF (Case Management/Electronic Case Files) system for electronic filing, which is only available to attorneys.
- Pro se filers cannot e-file their bankruptcy petitions—they must submit them in person or by mail.
- Consider using certified mail with a return receipt to verify that your documents are received by the court.

Key Steps to File for Bankruptcy Pro Se

Step 1: Gather Required Forms

- Download the bankruptcy forms from the U.S. Courts website (https://www.uscourts.gov/forms-rules/forms) or the Massachusetts Bankruptcy Court website (https://www.mab.uscourts.gov/forms).
- The key forms you'll need include:
  - Voluntary Petition (Form 101) – Officially declares your bankruptcy case.

- Schedules A/B, C, D, E/F, G, H, I, and J – Lists your assets, debts, income, expenses, and contracts.
- Means Test Form (Chapter 7 Only) – Determines if you qualify for Chapter 7 based on your income.

The means test isn't just about your income — it's about your disposable income after necessary living expenses. If your income is too high to qualify for Chapter 7, you may be required to file Chapter 13 instead.
Be honest and thorough with your expense reporting. The court can dismiss your case for abuse if it believes you're underreporting income or inflating expenses.

- Chapter 13 Plan Form – If filing for Chapter 13, outlines your repayment plan.
- Creditor Matrix – A list of all your creditors with contact information.

INSIGHT: In a Chapter 13 plan, you propose a repayment plan to pay off debts over 3 to 5 years. The judge will review whether your plan is feasible based on your income and reasonably structured. Your proposal must show how you will catch up on missed mortgage payments (if you want to keep the home) while maintaining payments for other necessary living expenses. You must demonstrate consistent income to support the plan — pay stubs, rental income, or other regular earnings.

If your income is irregular, you may need to include affidavits from employers, bank statements, or other documentation showing how you plan to maintain regular payments. The court is more likely to accept realistic, conservative plans rather than overly optimistic or inflated budgets.

Step 2: Complete the Credit Counseling Requirement

- Before filing, you must complete a court-approved credit counseling course within 180 days of your bankruptcy filing.
- Obtain the certificate of completion and include it with your petition.
- You can find approved agencies on the U.S. Trustee Program website: https://www.justice.gov/ust/list-credit-counseling-agencies-approved-pursuant-11-usc-111

Step 3: Pay the Filing Fee or Request a Fee Waiver

- Chapter 7 Standard Filing Fee: $338
- Chapter 13 Standard Filing Fee: $313
- If you cannot afford the fee, you can:
  - Apply for a fee waiver (Chapter 7 only).
  - Request to pay the fee in installments.

Step 4: Submit Your Petition and Obtain a Filing Receipt

Once you have completed your bankruptcy forms, you must submit your petition to the appropriate bankruptcy court in person or by mail.

Filing In Person (Recommended)

- If possible, it is strongly recommended to file your petition in person.
- When you file in person, ask the clerk for a filing receipt as proof that your case has been officially filed.
- This receipt contains the bankruptcy case number and filing date, which are critical for stopping foreclosure efforts.

Why the Filing Receipt Matters:

- The moment you file for bankruptcy, an automatic stay is triggered, which legally halts foreclosure proceedings.
- The filing receipt serves as evidence that your case is active.

Foreclosure Fight

- Immediately send a copy of the filing receipt to:
  - Your lender: This will notify them that the automatic stay is in effect, preventing them from proceeding with the foreclosure.
  - The attorney representing the lender.
  - Your attorney (if you have one): The attorney can use the receipt to formally notify the court and lender of your bankruptcy protection.
  - Use email, fax, or certified mail to send the receipt promptly, ensuring the lender receives it as soon as possible.
  - Consider following up by phone to confirm they received it.

Filing by Mail (If Necessary)

- If you must file by mail, include a self-addressed, stamped envelope with your submission.
- Request that the court return a stamped copy of your filing receipt.
- As soon as you receive the receipt, immediately send it to your lender and attorney to halt foreclosure efforts.

Extra Tip for Success: If you plan to reaffirm or "keep" certain debts like a car loan make sure you are current on those payments and can show that continuing to pay is within your budget.

Bankruptcy law allows you to:

- Reaffirm (continue paying a debt as if you never filed)
- Redeem (pay the current value of a secured asset in full — rarely used due to cash needed upfront)
- Surrender (return the item to the lender and discharge the debt)

Marc Saint Clair, MBA

Choose strategically. You are not obligated to keep every debt — many debtors surrender credit cards, second vehicles, or underwater investment properties.

Step 5: Attend the 341 Meeting of Creditors

- After filing, you will receive a notice of the 341 meeting (also called the creditors' meeting).
- You must attend this meeting and answer questions from the bankruptcy trustee about your finances and petition.
- Bring:
  - Photo ID (driver's license, passport, etc.).
  - Proof of Social Security number.
  - Bank statements, tax returns, and pay stubs (if requested).

Step 6: Complete the Debtor Education Course

- After filing, you must complete a Debtor Education Course to receive a discharge. This is a separate course from the pre-filing credit counseling course, which is required before submitting your bankruptcy petition:
- Website: https://www.justice.gov/ust/identify-your-countys-judicial-district
- Failing to complete this course can result in your case being closed without a discharge.

Key Tips for Pro Se Filers:

Double-Check Your Paperwork:

- Incomplete or inaccurate forms can lead to dismissal of your case.
- Double-check all forms for accuracy and completeness before submitting.

55

Foreclosure Fight

Keep Copies of Everything:

- Make copies of all documents before filing.
- Keep records of court notices, trustee correspondence, and proof of course completions.
- Draft a Cover Sheet or Summary Letter. This shows organization and helps court staff or trustees quickly understand your intent especially helpful in pro se filings.

Prepare for Objections or Challenges:

- Creditors or trustees may object to certain claims or challenge your eligibility.
- Understand that filing pro se makes you responsible for responding to motions and objections.
- Be Prepared for Trustee Questions. Trustees may ask: Why are certain luxury items or high expenses included? Are you making any non-essential payments (e.g., to family, subscriptions, donations)?

  Is your mortgage arrearage included in your Chapter 13 plan?
  Anticipate these questions and be prepared with explanations or documentation. The more organized and transparent you are, the more likely your plan will be confirmed.

Stay Organized and Meet Deadlines:

- Bankruptcy cases involve strict deadlines.
- Missing deadlines can result in the dismissal of your case.
- Use a calendar or reminder app to keep track of important dates.

Marc Saint Clair, MBA

Additional Resources for Pro Se Filers:

Massachusetts Legal Aid Programs:

- Volunteer Lawyers Project of Boston: www.vlpnet.org – Free legal aid for low-income residents.
- Massachusetts Legal Assistance Corporation (MLAC): www.mlac.org – Legal aid resources and referrals.

Self-Help Centers:

- The Massachusetts Bankruptcy Court offers self-help resources, including:
  - Bankruptcy filing guides.
  - Forms assistance.
  - Free or low-cost legal clinics.

Federal Resources:

- U.S. Courts Bankruptcy Basics: www.uscourts.gov – https://www.uscourts.gov/court-programs/bankruptcy/bankruptcy-basics Explains bankruptcy procedures for pro se filers.

Key Takeaway:
Filing for bankruptcy without an attorney is possible, but success depends on your preparation, honesty, and ability to follow instructions exactly. Beyond submitting paperwork, you must demonstrate financial stability, propose realistic repayment plans, and make strategic decisions about which debts to keep or discharge. Take full advantage of court resources, legal aid clinics, and self-help tools they can make all the difference in getting your plan accepted and your debts discharged.

Massachusetts General Laws on Foreclosure

Chapter 13
Chapter 244, Section
35A & 35B

Massachusetts General Laws Chapter 244, Section 35A

Section 35A: Right of residential real property borrower to cure a default; notice required to accelerate maturity of balance; contents of notice; late fees; filing

Section 35A. (a) Any borrower of residential real property located in the commonwealth, shall have a 90–day right to cure a default of a required payment as provided in such residential mortgage or note secured by such residential real property by full payment of all amounts that are due without acceleration of the maturity of the unpaid balance of such mortgage. The right to cure a default of a required payment shall be granted once during any 5–year period, regardless of the mortgage holder. For the purposes of this section, "residential property", shall mean real property located in the commonwealth having thereon a dwelling house with accommodations for 4 or less separate households and occupied, or to be occupied, in whole or in part by the borrower; provided, however, that residential property shall be limited to the principal residence of a person; provided further, that residential property shall not include an investment property or residence other than a primary residence; and provided further, that residential property shall not include residential property taken in whole or in part as collateral for a commercial loan.

(b) The mortgagee, or anyone holding thereunder, shall not accelerate maturity of the unpaid balance of such mortgage

Foreclosure Fight

obligation or otherwise enforce the mortgage because of a default consisting of the borrower's failure to make any such payment in subsection (a) by any method authorized by this chapter or any other law until at least 90 days after the date a written notice is given by the mortgagee to the borrower.

Said notice shall be deemed to be delivered to the borrower: (i) when delivered by hand to the borrower; or (ii) when sent by first class mail and certified mail or similar service by a private carrier to the borrower at the borrower's address last known to the mortgagee or anyone holding thereunder.

(c) The notice required in subsection (b) shall inform the borrower of the following:—

(1) the nature of the default claimed on such mortgage of residential real property and of the borrower's right to cure the default by paying the sum of money required to cure the default;

(2) the date by which the borrower shall cure the default to avoid acceleration, a foreclosure or other action to seize the home, which date shall not be less than 90 days after service of the notice and the name, address and local or toll free telephone number of a person to whom the payment or tender shall be made;

(3) that, if the borrower does not cure the default by the date specified, the mortgagee, or anyone holding thereunder, may take steps to terminate the borrower's ownership in the property by a foreclosure proceeding or other action to seize the home;

(4) the name and address of the mortgagee, or anyone holding thereunder, and the telephone number of a representative of the mortgagee whom the borrower may contact if the borrower disagrees with the mortgagee's assertion that a default has occurred or the correctness of the mortgagee's calculation of the amount required to cure the default;

(5) the name of any current and former mortgage broker or mortgage loan originator for such mortgage or note securing the residential property;

(6) that the borrower may be eligible for assistance from the Massachusetts Housing Finance Agency and the division of banks and the local or toll free telephone numbers the borrower may call to request this assistance;

(7) that the borrower may sell the property prior to the foreclosure sale and use the proceeds to pay off the mortgage;

(8) that the borrower may redeem the property by paying the total amount due, prior to the foreclosure sale;

(9) that the borrower may be evicted from the home after a foreclosure sale; and

(10) the borrower may have the following additional rights, depending on the terms of the residential mortgage: (i) to refinance the obligation by obtaining a loan which would fully repay the residential mortgage debtor; and (ii) to voluntarily grant a deed to the residential mortgage lender in lieu of foreclosure.

The notice shall also include a declaration, appearing on the first page of the notice stating: "This is an important notice concerning your right to live in your home. Have it translated at once."

The division of banks shall adopt regulations in accordance with this subsection.

(d) To cure a default prior to acceleration under this section, a borrower shall not be required to pay any charge, fee, or penalty attributable to the exercise of the right to cure a default. The borrower shall pay late fees as allowed pursuant to section 59 of chapter 183 and per-diem interest to cure such default. The borrower shall not be liable for any attorneys' fees relating to the borrower's default that are incurred by the mortgagee or anyone holding thereunder prior to or during the period set forth in the notice required by this section. The mortgagee, or anyone holding thereunder, may also provide for reinstatement of the note after the 90 day notice to cure has ended.

(e) A copy of the notice required by this section and an affidavit demonstrating compliance with this section shall be filed by the mortgagee, or anyone holding thereunder, in any action or proceeding to foreclose on such residential real property.

(f) A copy of the notice required by this section shall also be filed by the mortgagee, or anyone holding thereunder, with the commissioner of the division of banks. Additionally, if the residential property securing the mortgage loan is sold at a foreclosure sale, the mortgagee, or anyone holding thereunder, shall notify the commissioner of the division of banks, in writing, of the date of the foreclosure sale and the purchase price obtained at the sale.

Massachusetts General Laws Chapter 244, Section 35B - Requirement of reasonable steps and good faith effort to avoid foreclosure; criteria; notice of right to pursue modified mortgage; recording of affidavit of compliance.

Section 35B. (a) As used in this section, the following words shall, unless the context clearly requires otherwise, have the following meanings:—

"Affordable monthly payment", monthly payments on a mortgage loan, which, taking into account the borrower's current circumstances, including verifiable income, debts, assets and obligations enable a borrower to make the payments.

"Borrower", a mortgagor of a mortgage loan.

"Certain mortgage loan", a loan to a natural person made primarily for personal, family or household purposes secured wholly or partially by a mortgage on an owner-occupied residential property with 1 or more of the following loan features: (i) an introductory interest rate granted for a period of 3 years or less and such introductory rate is at least 2 per cent lower than the fully indexed rate; (ii) interest-only payments for any period of time, except in the case where the mortgage loan is an open-end home equity line of credit or is a construction loan; (iii) a payment option feature, where any 1 of the payment options is less than principal and interest fully amortized over the life of the loan; (iv) the loan did not require full documentation of income or assets; (v) prepayment penalties that exceed section 56 of chapter 183 or applicable federal law; (vi) the loan was underwritten with a loan-to-value ratio at or above 90 per cent and the ratio of the borrower's debt, including all housing-related and recurring monthly debt, to the borrower's income exceeded 38 per cent; or (vii) the loan was underwritten as a component of a loan transaction, in which the combined loan-to-value ratio exceeded 95 per cent; provided, however, that a loan shall be a certain mortgage loan if, after the performance of reasonable due diligence, a creditor is unable to determine whether the loan has 1 or more of the loan features in clauses (i) to (vii), inclusive; and provided, further, that loans financed by the Massachusetts Housing Finance Agency, established in chapter 708 of the acts of 1966 and loans originated through programs administered by the Massachusetts Housing Partnership Fund board established in section 35 of chapter 405 of the acts of 1985 shall not be certain mortgage loans.

"Creditor", a person or entity that holds or controls, partially, wholly, indirectly, directly or in a nominee capacity, a mortgage loan securing an owner-occupied residential property, including, but not limited to, an originator, holder, investor, assignee, successor, trust, trustee, nominee holder, Mortgage Electronic Registration System or mortgage servicer, including the Federal National Mortgage Association or the Federal Home Loan Mortgage Corporation; provided, that "creditor" shall also include any servant, employee or agent of a creditor; and provided, further, that the bodies politic and corporate and public instrumentalities of the commonwealth established in chapter 708 of the acts of 1966 and in section 35 of chapter 405 of the acts of 1985 shall not be a creditor.

"Creditor's representative", a person who has the authority to negotiate and approve the terms of and modify a mortgage loan, or a person who, under a servicing agreement, has the authority to negotiate and approve the terms of and modify a mortgage loan.

"Modified mortgage loan", a mortgage loan modified from its original terms including, but not limited to, a loan modified under 1 of the following: (i) the Home Affordable Modification Program; (ii) the Federal Deposit Insurance Corporation's Loan Modification Program; (iii) any modification program that a lender uses which is based on accepted principles and the safety and soundness of the institution and authorized by the National Credit Union Administration, the division of banks or any other instrumentality of the commonwealth; (iv) the Federal Housing Administration; or (v) a similar federal loan modification plan.

"Mortgage loan", a loan to a natural person made primarily for personal, family or household purposes secured wholly or partially by a mortgage on residential property.

"Net present value", the present net value of a residential property based on a calculation using 1 of the following: (i) the federal Home Affordable Modification Program base net present value model; (ii) the Federal Deposit Insurance Corporation's Loan Modification Program; (iii) the Massachusetts Housing Finance Agency's loan program used solely by the agency to compare the expected economic outcome of a loan with or without a modified mortgage loan; or (iv) any model approved by the division of banks to consider the total present value of a series of future cash flows relative to a mortgage loan.

"Residential property", real property located in the commonwealth, on which there is a dwelling house with accommodations for 4 or fewer separate households and occupied, or to be occupied, in whole or in part by the obligor on the mortgage debt; provided, however, that residential property shall be limited to the principal residence of a person; provided, further, that residential property shall not include an investment property or residence other than a primary residence; provided, further, that residential property shall not include residential property taken in whole or in part as collateral for a commercial loan; and provided, further, that residential property shall not include a property subject to condemnation or receivership.

(b) A creditor shall not cause publication of notice of a foreclosure sale, as required by section 14, upon certain mortgage loans unless it has first taken reasonable steps and made a good faith effort to avoid foreclosure. A creditor shall have taken reasonable steps and made a good faith effort to avoid foreclosure if the creditor has considered: (i) an assessment of the borrower's ability to make an affordable monthly payment; (ii) the net present value of receiving payments under a modified mortgage loan as compared to the anticipated net recovery following foreclosure; and (iii) the interests of the creditor, including, but not limited to, investors.

(1) Except as otherwise specified in a contract, a servicer of pooled residential mortgages may determine whether the net present value of the payments on the modified mortgage loan is likely to be greater than the anticipated net recovery that would result from foreclosure to all investors and holders of beneficial interests in such investment, but not to any individual or groups of investors or beneficial interest holders. The servicer shall act in the best interests of all such investors or holders of beneficial interests if the servicer agrees to or implements a modified mortgage loan or takes reasonable loss mitigation actions that comply with this section. Any modified mortgage loan offered to the borrower shall comply with current federal and state law, including, but not limited to, all rules and regulations pertaining to mortgage loans and the borrower shall be able to reasonably afford to repay the modified mortgage loan according to its scheduled payments. Notwithstanding section 63A of chapter 183, any modified mortgage loan may be made without the consent of the holders of junior encumbrances and without loss of priority for the full amount of the loan thereby

modified and shall not be construed so as to grant to any such holder of a junior encumbrance rights which, except for said revision, the holder would not otherwise have.

(2) A creditor shall be presumed to have acted in good faith and to have complied with this subsection, if, prior to causing publication of notice of a foreclosure sale, as required by section 14, the creditor:

(i) determines a borrower's current ability to make an affordable monthly payment;

(ii) identifies a modified mortgage loan that achieves the borrower's affordable monthly payment, which may include 1 or more of the following: reduction in principal, reduction in interest rate or an increase in amortization period; provided, however, that the amortization period shall not be more than a 15–year increase; provided, further, that no modified mortgage loan shall have an amortization period that exceeds 45 years;

(iii) conducts a compliant analysis comparing the net present value of the modified mortgage loan and the creditor's anticipated net recovery that would result from foreclosure; provided, that the analysis shall be compliant if the analysis is in accordance with the formula presented in at least 1 of the following: (A) the Home Affordable Modification Program; (B) the Federal Deposit Insurance Corporation's Loan Modification Program; (C) any modification program that a lender uses which is based on accepted principles and the safety and soundness of the institution and authorized by the National Credit Union Administration, the division of banks or any other instrumentality of the commonwealth; (D) the Federal Housing Administration; or (E) a similar federal loan modification plan; and

(iv) either (A) in all circumstances where the net present value of the modified mortgage loan exceeds the anticipated net recovery at foreclosure, agrees to modify the loan in a manner that provides for the affordable monthly payment; or (B) in circumstances where the net present value of the modified mortgage loan is less than the anticipated net recovery of the foreclosure, or does not meet the borrower's affordable monthly payment, notifies the borrower that no modified mortgage loan will be offered and provides a written summary of the creditor's net present value analysis and the borrower's current ability to make monthly payments, after which the creditor may proceed with the foreclosure process in conformity with this chapter.

(c) Under this section, for certain mortgage loans, the creditor shall send notice, concurrently with the notice required by subsection (g) of section 35A, of the borrower's rights to pursue a modified mortgage loan. Said notice shall be considered delivered to the borrower when sent by first class mail and certified mail or similar service by a private carrier to the borrower at the borrower's address last known to the mortgagee or anyone holding thereunder. A copy of said notice shall be filed with the attorney general. The process for determining whether a modified mortgage loan is offered shall take no longer than 150 days. Not more than 30 days following delivery of the notice as provided for in this subsection, a borrower who holds a certain mortgage loan shall notify a creditor of: (i) the borrower's intent to pursue a modified mortgage loan which shall include a statement of the borrower's income and a complete list of total debts and obligations, as requested by the creditor, at the time of receipt of the notice; (ii) the borrower's intent to pursue an alternative to foreclosure, including a short sale or deed-in-lieu of foreclosure; (iii) the borrower's intent not to pursue a modified mortgage loan and pursue the right to cure period described in section 35A; or (iv) the borrower's intent to waive the right to cure period and proceed to foreclosure. A borrower who holds a certain mortgage loan and fails to respond to the creditor within 30 days of delivery of the notice provided for in this subsection shall be considered to have forfeited the right to cure period and shall be subject to a right to cure period of 90 days. A borrower shall be presumed to have notified the creditor if the borrower provides proof of delivery through the United States Postal Service or similar carrier. Not more than 30 days following receipt of the borrower's notification that the borrower intends to pursue a modified mortgage loan, a creditor shall provide the borrower with its assessment, in writing, under subsection (b). The assessment shall include, but not be limited to: (i) a written statement of the borrower's income, debts and obligations as determined by the creditor; (ii) the creditor's net present value analysis of the mortgage loan; (iii) the creditor's anticipated net recovery at foreclosure; (iv) a statement of the interests of the creditor; and (v) a modified mortgage loan offer under the requirements of this section or notice that no modified mortgage loan will be offered. If a creditor offers a modified mortgage loan, the offer shall include the first and last names and contact phone numbers of the creditor's representative; provided, that the creditor shall not assign more than 2 creditor's representatives responsible for negotiating and approving the terms of and modifying the mortgage loan. The assessment shall be provided by first class and certified mail. A creditor shall be presumed to have provided the assessment to the borrower if the creditor provides proof of delivery through the United States Postal Service or similar carrier. A borrower who receives a modified mortgage loan offer from a creditor shall respond within 30 days of receipt of the assessment and offer of a modified mortgage loan. The borrower may: (i) accept the offer of a loan modification as provided by the creditor; (ii) make a reasonable counteroffer; or (iii) state that the borrower wishes to waive the borrower's rights as provided by this section and proceed to foreclosure. The borrower's response shall be in writing and, if a counteroffer is proposed, shall include substantiating documentation in support of the counteroffer. The response shall be provided by first class and certified mail. A borrower shall be presumed to have responded if the borrower provides proof of delivery through the United States Postal Service or similar carrier. A borrower who fails to respond to the creditor within 30 days of receipt of a modified mortgage loan offer shall be considered to have forfeited the 150 day right to cure period and shall be subject to a right to cure period of 90 days. Where a counteroffer is proposed, the creditor shall accept, reject or propose a counteroffer to the borrower within 30 days of receipt. Under this section, additional offers by both parties shall be considered during the right to cure period; provided, however, that a borrower may at any time state, in writing, that the borrower wishes to waive the borrower's rights as provided by this section and proceed to foreclosure. Nothing in this section shall be construed as preventing a creditor and a borrower from negotiating the terms of a modified mortgage loan by telephone or in person following the initial offer of a modified mortgage loan by a creditor; provided, however, that all offers, whether by a creditor or a borrower, shall be in writing and signed by the offeror. The right to a modified mortgage loan, as described in this section, shall be granted once during any 3–year period, regardless of the mortgage holder.

(d) The notice required in subsection (c) shall, at a minimum, include the appropriate contact information for modification assistance within the office of the attorney general; provided, that, the notice shall be similar in substance and form to the notice promulgated by the division of banks under section 35A.

(e) Nothing in this section shall prevent a creditor from offering or accepting an alternative to foreclosure, such as a short sale or deed-in-lieu of foreclosure, if the borrower requests such alternative, rejects a modified mortgage loan offer or does not qualify for a modified mortgage loan under this section.

(f) Prior to publishing a notice of a foreclosure sale, as required by section 14, the creditor, or if the creditor is not a natural person, an officer or duly authorized agent of the creditor, shall certify compliance with this section in an affidavit based upon a review of the creditor's business records. The creditor, or an officer or duly authorized agent of the creditor, shall record this affidavit with the registry of deeds for the county or district where the land lies.

The affidavit certifying compliance with this section shall be conclusive evidence in favor of an arm's-length third party purchaser for value, at or subsequent to the resulting foreclosure sale, that the creditor has fully complied with this section and the mortgagee is entitled to proceed with foreclosure of the subject mortgage under the power of sale contained in the mortgage and any 1 or more of the foreclosure procedures authorized in this chapter; provided, that the arm's-length third party purchaser for value relying on such affidavit shall not be liable for any failure of the foreclosing party to comply and title to the real property thereby acquired shall not be set aside on account of such failure. The filing of such affidavit shall not relieve the affiant, or other person on whose behalf the affidavit is executed, from liability for failure to comply with this section, including by reason of any statement in the affidavit. For purposes of this subsection, the term "arm's-length, third party purchaser for value" shall include such purchaser's heirs, successors and assigns.

(g) On a bi-annual basis, a creditor shall report the final outcome of each loan modification on all mortgage loans for which the creditor sent to a borrower a notice of the right to pursue a modified mortgage loan to the division of banks.

(h) The division of banks shall adopt, amend or repeal regulations to aid in the administration and enforcement of this section, including the minimum requirements which constitute a good faith effort by the borrower to respond to the notice required under subsection (c); provided, that, such regulations may include requirements for reasonable steps and good faith efforts of the creditor to avoid foreclosure and safe harbors for compliance in addition to those under this section. The division of banks shall make any available net present value models accessible to all creditors.

Chapter 14
Foreclosure Related Fees

Massachusetts General Laws Chapter 183, Section 59

Massachusetts General Laws Chapter 183, Section **59** specifically covers **foreclosure-related fees** and **penalties** for residential mortgages. It provides important **consumer protections** against excessive or unfair late fees.

Section 59. A mortgagee, assignee or holder of a mortgage note secured by a first or subordinate lien on a dwelling house of 4 or less separate households or on a residential condominium unit occupied or to be occupied in whole or in part by the mortgagor shall not require the mortgagor to pay a late charge or late payment penalty unless the penalty is specifically authorized in the loan documents.

A mortgagee, assignee or holder of a mortgage note secured by a first or subordinate lien on a dwelling house of 4 or less separate households or on a residential condominium unit occupied or to be occupied in whole or in part by the mortgagor shall not require the mortgagor to pay a penalty or late charge for any payment paid within 15 days or in the case of a bi-weekly mortgage payment, paid within 10 days, from the date the payment is due.

In no event, in assessing a penalty because of the delinquency in making all or any part of a periodic payment under a mortgage note, shall the penalty or late charge exceed 3 per cent of the amount of principal and interest overdue, and in calculating the penalty or late charge, any amount of the periodic payment representing estimated tax payments required by the terms of the mortgage note or deed shall not be included.

A late payment penalty or late charge may not be charged more than once with respect to a single late payment. If a late payment fee is deducted from a payment made on the loan, and the deduction causes a subsequent default on a subsequent payment, no late payment fee may be imposed for the default. If a late payment fee has been once imposed with respect to a particular late payment, a fee shall not be imposed with respect to any future payment which would have been timely and sufficient, but for the previous default.

Conclusion

In closing this book, my greatest hope is that it serves as a beacon of knowledge and empowerment for anyone facing the challenge of foreclosure. Regardless of your background, financial status, or circumstances, you deserve to be equipped with the tools, rights, and resources necessary to protect your home and secure your future.

Foreclosure is not merely a legal or financial event—it is a deeply personal experience that can uproot lives and destabilize families. However, by understanding the laws, protections, and strategies outlined in this book, you can approach the process with confidence and clarity. Whether you are fighting to save your home, seeking loan modifications, or exploring foreclosure prevention programs, knowledge is your most powerful ally.

My hope is that this book not only guides you through the complexities of foreclosure but also inspires you to advocate for fair and just housing practices. By sharing this knowledge with others, you contribute to building stronger, more informed, and resilient communities—where homeownership remains an attainable dream, not a fleeting privilege.